Chickens

by Peter Brady

FRANKLIN WATTS

NEW YORK • LONDON • SYDNEY

This edition first published in 1998

Franklin Watts
96 Leonard Street
London EC2A 4RH

Franklin Watts Australia
14 Mars Road
Lane Cove
NSW 2066

Original edition published in the United States by Capstone Press
818 North Willow Street, Mankato, Minnesota 56001
Copyright © 1996, 1998 by Capstone Press

ISBN 0 7496 3200 3
Dewey Decimal Classification Number: 636.5

A CIP catalogue record for this book is available from the British Library.

Printed in Belgium

Photographs
All the photographs were taken by William Muñoz.

Contents

Words in the text in **bold** type are explained in the Useful words section on page 23.

What is a chicken?

A chicken is a bird.
Sometimes we call it 'poultry'.
In every country of the world
people keep chickens
for their eggs and their meat.
Today, most chickens are kept on farms.

Cockerels and hens

Male chickens are called
cockerels or cocks.
A cockerel has a red **comb**
on top of his head,
and **wattles** hanging below his beak.
Female chickens are called hens.
They lay eggs.

What chickens look like

Chickens have plump bodies,
silky feathers and two strong feet.
They have wings too,
but cannot fly very well.
Chickens can be striped, spotted
or just one colour.
Hens weigh between one and six kilos.
Cockerels often weigh more.

Where chickens live

Chickens usually live in
a henhouse or chicken **coop**.
A henhouse should have an outside run,
because chickens like to scratch
the ground to find food.

What chickens eat

Chickens eat grain
and special chicken food.
When they scratch the ground
they are looking for seeds,
insects and grass.
They will also eat scraps of food
like bread and potatoes.

Different kinds of chicken

People have been keeping chickens
for hundreds of years.
Now there are more than
50 different **breeds**.
The names of some of them are
Rhode Island Red, Leghorn, Cornish,
Ancona and Wyandotte.

Eggs

One hen can lay
between 60 and 150 eggs a year.
The eggs can be white,
brown or speckled.
If the eggs are not **fertilized**,
they can be used for cooking and eating.

Chicks

If the eggs are fertilized,
they can become chicks.
Hens sit on the fertilized eggs
for three weeks.
This keeps the eggs warm
so the chick inside each one can develop.
When the chicks are ready to **hatch**,
they break out of the shells.

What chickens give us

Chickens give us eggs and meat.
Chicken is one of the most popular foods
all over the world.
In the past, country people
used chicken feathers
to fill cushions and bedding.
Today most fillings are man-made.

Why you shouldn't count your chickens

A milkmaid was going to market with a bucket of milk balanced on her head. As she walked she started planning.

With the money from the milk, she would buy a dozen eggs. The eggs would hatch and she would sell the chickens and buy a beautiful dress. The dress would make everyone jealous, but she would just stick her nose in the air.

As she thought this, she stuck her nose in the air and the bucket fell off her head. All her plans were now just a puddle on the ground.

The moral of the story is: do not count your chickens before they hatch.

(from a tale by Aesop)

Useful words

breed group of animals with the same ancestors
coop small cage or run in which chickens are kept
comb red growth on the top of a chicken's head.
Cockerels have bigger combs than hens
fertilized an egg laid after a cockerel and hen have
come together to produce chicks
hatch when a chick leaves its egg
wattles loose flaps of skin hanging from each side of a
cockerel's face

Books to read

Burton, Robert, *Egg*, Dorling Kindersley, 1994
Legg, Gerald, *Lifecycles: From Egg to Chicken*, Watts, 1997
See How They Grow: Chick, Dorling Kindersley, 1993
Wallace, Karen, *My Hen is Dancing*, Walker Books, 1993

Index

Ancona 15

beak 7
bread 13
breeds 13

chicks 19

cockerels 7, 9
comb 7
cooking 17
coop 11
Cornish 15

eggs 5, 7, 17, 19, 21

farms 5
feathers 9, 21
fertilized 17, 19
food 11

grain 13
grass 13

hatch 19

henhouse 11
hens 7, 9, 17, 19

insects 13

Leghorn 15

meat 5, 21

Rhode Island Red 15

seeds 13
shell 19

wattles 7
Wyandotte 15

PRINTED IN BELGIUM BY
proost
INTERNATIONAL BOOK PRODUCTION